Legends of Rock & Roll

The Bee Gees

An unauthorized fan tribute

By: James Hoag

Paperback Edition

Other Paperbacks by James Hoag

Legends of Rock and Roll Series

Legends of Rock & Roll Volume 1 - The Fifties

Legends of Rock & Roll Volume 2 - The Sixties

Legends of Rock & Roll Volume 3 - The Seventies

The Beatles

Queen

Individual Beatles

John Lennon

Paul McCartney

George Harrison

Ringo Starr

Fifties

Everly Brothers

Sixties

Neil Diamond

Roy Orbison

The Beach Boys

Bob Dylan

The Doors

Seventies

Eagles

Eighties

Madonna

Legends of Country Music

Reba McEntire

Willie Nelson

Johnny Cash

George Jones

Merle Haggard

Garth Brooks

Waylon Jennings

(All Available at Amazon.com)

Table of Contents

INTRODUCTION

Do you know what I liked best about the British Invasion of the Sixties? I liked everything. I loved the Beatles and the Stones and Herman's Hermits and the Dave Clark Five. But one of my favorites has always been The Bee Gees.

I even liked the Bee Gees when they first started in the Sixties. But when they reinvented themselves in the Seventies and became Disco Gods, I really sat up and took notice. If you haven't watched "Saturday Night Fever" lately, go rent it or get it from Netflix or buy it. Just get it and watch it. John Travolta did a decent job in the movie, but, in my opinion, the music is the star of the show. And most of that music is done by the Bee Gees.

We have a few family acts that have made it big in the world of Rock and Roll, like the Jacksons and the Osmonds. But, no one can stand up to the Bee Gees. Like the Osmonds and Jacksons, these guys were all brothers, had grown up together and could harmonize. Oh, could they harmonize. From their early hits like "How Do You Mend a Broken Heart" to their Disco years, "Jive Talking' and "Staying Alive", the Bee Gees made a mark on the world of Rock and Roll that is still felt today.

The Bee Gees had two distinct periods of popularity. They did pretty well in the Sixties when the British Invasion was at its peak. Then, about 1972, they sort of drifted away and we didn't hear from them for 3 years. In 1975, they re-invented themselves and became Disco kings.

Two of the three are now gone. I mourn their passing because they left us way too early. I remember thinking when John Lennon was killed, "there will never be another performance of the Beatles". I felt the same way about the Bee Gees when Maurice passed away in 2003.

If you love the Bee Gees, I hope you enjoy my tribute to the Brothers Gibb.

THE BROTHERS GROWING UP

The Gibb Family had five children. Mom was Barbara May Pass and Dad was Hugh Gibb. Hughie (as he was called) was a professional drummer and leader of his own band during the early Forties. He and his band would play different venues and dance halls. One night in Manchester, he spotted a pretty girl who had come to listen to the music. He was immediately smitten and one thing led to another and he and Barbara May were married. Barbara actually worked as his vocalist until the first child came.

On January 12, 1945, Lesley Evans was born in Manchester, England, where Hughie was playing at the time. Hughie next got a job on the Isle of Man, so the little family moved there to Douglass, the capital of the island.

Barry was born Barry Alan Crompton Gibb on September 1, 1946. When Barry was about two years old, he was badly burned. His mother had set a pot of boiling tea on the table and young Barry reached for it and scalded himself. He was immediately taken to the hospital where he would spend two and a half months. At one point, no one was sure if he would live. But, of course, he did and he says today that he doesn't remember it at all. But the scars are still present.

Three years later, on December 22, 1949 twin boys Robin Hugh Gibb and Maurice (pronounced "Morris") Ernest Gibb were welcomed into the family. Mother, Barbara, was pretty sure she was having twins. She told her friends that she had had a premonition. This was before ultra sounds and other medical devices that can determine gender of a baby. But the doctor had told her that he heard two heart beats so they were expecting twins.

Robin is actually the oldest, being born about 35 minutes before Maurice. There were now four children in the family with Barry stuck in the middle between an older sister and two younger brothers. This did cause him some initial jealousy, but he soon accepted the new boys as part of the family.

The family moved several times while in Douglass. Then in 1953, they moved to Chorlton-cum-Hardy in Manchester, England. Barry was seven years old and the twins were about five. They attended Oswald Road Primary School. It was here that they learned that they could sing and harmonize with each other. They would sing for their friends and at school.

This was about eight years after the end of World War II and Manchester still showed the signs of war. There were buildings that had not been replaced after being bombed. The boys found all of this a never ending source of interest and mischief.

Barry had difficulty adjusting to his new school. It is said that the head master did not like him and tried to make his life miserable. He became so afraid to go to school, that he actually stopped going for a while, not telling his parents.

The twins were in trouble all of the time. Robin liked to set fires. Maurice tried shoplifting once but got caught and that was the end of that

Since Dad was a drummer and had his own band, it's not surprising that the boys grew up listening to music. Their older sister Lesley liked to listen to Rock and Roll on the radio and the boys soon became fans as well. They made their own instruments and pretended to play. They would sing along with the radio.

A cute story is told of the boys signing up to perform at the local cinema. They were going to lip-sync to a song. Sounds like a Fifties version of karaoke. The three were running toward the theater when one of them dropped the 78 rpm record that they were planning to play and it broke. Well, now they had a problem. So, they decided to do the song live. The crowd loved it and a spark was lit that would grow to be a successful career for the three boys.

Dad noticed, too and thought he might have something special in his three boys. He couldn't have been more right. He got them a one-night stand at a local club in Manchester called the Russell Street Club, where his band played. It was an adult club and minors really weren't allowed, so Dad smuggled them in through the back door and they were able to sing before a live audience. They actually got paid for singing and now at about nine and six years old, they were professionals.

They called themselves various names, including The Rattlesnakes and Wee Johnny Hays and the Blue Cats.

MOVING TO AUSTRALIA

In 1958, after a break of nine years between children, the Gibb family had their fifth child, a boy, Andrew Roy Gibb, born on March 5. Andy would grow up to have his own career and actually compete with his brothers for the attention of the record buying public. Barry was eleven and his twin brothers were nine. Mom Barbara's sister, Audrey, decided to immigrate to Australia and Barbara thought that might be a good idea for the Gibb family. So that same year, the family moved again; this time to Brisbane, Australia.

If you think about moving to Australia, you might assume that they shipped all their stuff and got on a plane and flew there. Nope, they loaded all of their possessions on a boat and for 20 pounds, they bought their fare to Australia. The trip took five weeks.

During the voyage, they continued to practice their singing. They would sit in the bow of the ship and people would gather around to listen. On the ship they were known as Barry and the Twins. They arrived in Sydney, Australia on September 1, 1958 which was Barry's twelfth birthday. They didn't stay in Sydney, but migrated north to Brisbane.

They settled in Redcliffe, Queensland which is just north of Brisbane and on the eastern coast of Australia. I just put it on my bucket list of places I want to see before I die. Barry began almost immediately to perform wherever he and his brothers could. They called themselves the Rattlesnakes.

There was a racetrack nearby called the Redcliffe Speedway. The boys approached the manager and asked if they could play between races. Why not, the manager said and so, Barry with his guitar and the twins backing him up, they started putting on small shows to entertain the crowd between races. They didn't get paid, but people would throw money onto the track and they could pick that up. It was a start.

Barry was twelve and Maurice and Robin were nine.

After a year of doing this and performing everywhere else they could, a race car driver named Bill Goode noticed them and noticed how excited the crowd got when they came on stage. Goode knew a Disc Jockey from Sydney named Bill Gates (not *the* Bill Gates) and asked him to hear the boys. Gates was impressed. He recognized right away that they were young and inexperienced, but they could sing.

Bill Gates became their promoter and began to play their songs on his radio program. People listened and wanted to know where they could buy their records. Of course, there were no records. First they needed a name. You may have figured out by now that they were surrounded by people with the initials BG. There was Bill Goode, the race car driver, Bill Gates, the disc jockey and of course, Barry Gibb, himself. Also, the Brothers Gibb would be BG. So, that's what their name was in the beginning, the BG's. It wasn't until about 1963 that they expanded it and became the Bee Gees.

THE BEE GEES ARE BORN

Bill Gates didn't last very long as their promoter. He was a disc jockey, not a businessman, so the job was taken over by the boy's dad, Hugh. Like he did in England, he started getting them jobs in local nightclubs and other venues. He had to drive them because they were too young to drive. Several trips required them to miss school and they had to get the head masters permission to do so.

Barry started writing songs. One of the first was called "Time Is Passing By". Just for fun, I searched YouTube for the song, not really expecting to find it, but there it was. If you would like to see the Brothers Gibb when they were about nine to twelve years old, you can see them on YouTube. Just search for Bee Gees Time Is Passing By. They performed on what looks like a local TV station in Brisbane.

A performer in England, Tommy Steele, who is considered to be Britain's first teen idol recorded "Time Is Passing By" in 1960, making it the first time a Bee Gees song was covered by someone else.

Other songs Barry wrote early on were "Turtle Dove", "Twenty Miles to Blueland" and "Let Me Love You". They were pretty young to be writing and singing love songs, but they pulled it off. Couldn't find the first song, but clips of the latter two songs can be found on YouTube if you'd like to give them a listen.

By 1960, they were playing on several television shows, thanks to their dad. They did not have a record contract yet at this point. That was about to change. The family was still living in Brisbane in 1960 and Dad took the boys around to every television show he could find. They appeared on a program called "Brisbane Tonight" and another one called "Strictly for Moderns". Now these appearances didn't make them stars but it did get them noticed by the public. People were talking about the Bee Gees.

They became popular enough that they were asked to be regulars on a local program called "Cottee's Happy Hour" which was a variety show sponsored by a soft drink company called Cottee. They would sing standards from the Forties like "Bye Bye Blackbird" and "Dinah", but they also sang their own songs, most of which Barry had written.

Barry continued to write. Many of his songs were recorded by other Australian artists. One, in particular, a fellow by the name of Col Joye had a big hit with one of Barry's compositions, "Underneath the Starlight of Love". Joye was one of the early rock and roll performers in Australia. He was the first rock and roll artist to have a number one hit in Australia.

In 1961, Barry would have been about 15 years old. He knew that his future lie in music and so he dropped out of High School. Two years later, Maurice and Robin followed him by also dropping out. They had to make it, now. The boys enjoyed performing in and around Brisbane, but wanted the big time. They wanted to go to Sydney. So, they moved in that direction by playing in hotels and clubs that ran along the eastern coast of Australia about 45 miles from Brisbane.

In 1966, Barry met Maureen Bates, a native of Sydney. They were married shortly after meeting on August 22, 1966, but the relationship was bad right from the beginning. Someone said that they were looking for safety and security in the marriage and just the opposite happened. The marriage was like a prison for them. Two years later, after meeting model Linda Gray, Barry and Maureen separated and eventually divorced in 1970.

WORKING THEIR WAY UP

They were staying at a hotel on the east coast of Australia called the Surfer's Paradise, when they discovered that Col Joye was staying there, also. Barry decided to take matters into his own hands and knocked on Joye's door. He handed Joye a recording of one of their songs and asked him to listen to it. Joye said he would and soon called the boys and asked them to come to Sydney.

This was the answer to their dream. They were about to enter the big time. Soon, the whole family had moved to Sydney and, in 1963, the Bee Gees signed a record contract with the Festival Records subsidiary Leedon Records.

They wasted no time in putting out a single. "The Battle of the Blue and the Gray" was released in March of 1963. It was only released in Australia, but unfortunately, it did not chart. The record was produced by Col Joye, which shows how much confidence he had in the guys. They used Joye's backup band, called the Joy Boys, as their backup.

For the next couple years, they recorded and wrote songs. Barry was so prolific that he was able to write for his own group and for many other performers as well. In 1965, they released their first album called "The Bee Gees Sing and Play 14 Barry Gibb Songs". A long name for a first album. It was only released in Australia, but did very well for a first album.

The album was basically a collection of singles which Barry had written over the past three years as they were getting their feet on the ground. The album itself did not chart, not even in Australia, but did produce a couple singles which hit the Australian Top 100. A song that previously had been released as a single in 1963, "Timber", peaked at number 75 on the Australian charts. Their breakthrough came when, in 1965, "Wine and Women" reached number 19 on the charts.

For a short time in 1964, the boys had their own television show in Sydney. Because of the success they were having, radio station 5KA in Adelaide, Australia named Barry Gibb composer of the year. Pretty good for a nineteen year old.

Their second album, recorded under the Spin label was originally called "Monday's Rain", but when the single "Spicks and Specks" was released in Australia in 1966, it rocketed to number five on the local charts. They quickly changed the name of the album to "Spicks and Specks" and they had a hit on their hands.

MOVING BACK TO ENGLAND

Sensing that they now had a future in the music business, on November 25, 1966, the family packed up their belongings and took a ship back to England. Hugh and Barbara didn't want to go back to England. They hadn't liked it that much the first time around. Hugh even threatened to hide the boy's passports to prevent the trip, but in the end, he gave in and off they went. It was a six week trip to England aboard a ship. There was not much to do, so the boys performed for the other passengers and wrote songs. They had quite a few done by the time they arrived. I read that the majority of the song "To Love Somebody" (which charted in 1967) was written during this trip. The song was later finished when they got to England.

They immediately went on tour through the British Isles. The single "Spicks and Specks" was released to the rest of the world in February of 1967. It did not chart in the U.S. or in England, but it hit number two in the Netherlands and number one in New Zealand.

Just before leaving for England, their dad, Hugh sent demo tapes to Brian Epstein. You probably remember that Epstein was the manager of the Beatles at the time, so Hugh was starting at the top. Epstein liked what he heard and passed the tapes to Robert Stigwood. Stigwood was also from Australia and maybe Epstein thought he could relate better to the guys.

Stigwood met with the three and immediately liked what he heard. He told them to go collect their guitars (still being stored from the trip) and come back and play for him. They did and a few hours later, he offered them a five year contract. From first meeting with Stigwood until the signing of the contract was less than one day.

I have been calling them boys, but from that moment on, they were men. The Bee Gees were to become one of the greatest groups to come out of England during the Sixties, probably second only to the Beatles. The icing on the cake was that that was the day Robin met Molly Hullis, who was Stigwood's secretary. Molly remembers when the group first walked into Stegwood's office. "Here comes trouble." she thought. She was not impressed.

Robin and Molly would later be married in 1968 and have two children, Spencer (born 1972) and Melissa (born 1974), before divorcing in 1980.

The contract would allow the group to record on Polydor Records in England and Atco Records in the United States.

"NEW YORK MINING DISASTER 1941"

"New York Mining Disaster 1941" was the first single released under the new contract. It was released with a blank label. Only the name of the song was printed. No artist given. The radio stations all assumed it was a new Beatles song and so it got played a lot. The ruse was discovered after a time, but by then the song had entered the Top 20 in both England and in the United States.

Even when the public found out the song was by the Bee Gees, they thought the Beatles were just playing under another name. Other bands had done that, why not the Beatles. But, of course, we know it was not the Beatles, but the three brothers from Australia, the Bee Gees.

Barry and Robin wrote "New York Mining Disaster 1941" while sitting in the dark at the Polydor Studios pretending they were trapped underground in a mine collapse. I'm not sure why they dated it 1941, because the song is based on a mining disaster that happened in the Welch village of Aberfan in 1966. Because of water buildup at the mine, a slide dumped tons of shale and rock upon the town, burying a nearby school. 166 children were killed along with 28 adults.

When writing the song, they imagined what it would be like to be buried underground with no hope of rescue. If you listen carefully to the song, the 2nd verse is slower than the first and the third verse is slower than the 2nd. This is to imply that the men are slowly dying and hope is fading.

The song peaked at number 14 in the U.S. and number 12 in England. So, after working hard for seven or eight years, they were over-night sensations and on their way to stardom.

"TO LOVE SOMEBODY"

Next they released "To Love Somebody". No tricks were played in the release of this song. By then, everyone knew the Bee Gees and they did not have to pretend anymore. The song is really a blues song and was originally written for Otis Redding. I would dearly love to hear what Otis would have done with this song, but he died before he had a chance to record it.

So, the guys recorded it themselves and it became their second hit. It didn't do as well in England, peaking at only number 41. In the U.S., it reached the Top 20, peaking at number 17. Barry mentioned that he didn't think the song was right for England because it is really a soul song. But people in the United States loved it. Michael Bolton would cover the song in 1993, but only reached number 83 on the Billboard Top 100.

Between "To Love Somebody" and their third hit "Holiday", the guys released their third album. It was the first to be recorded in England under the Polydor label, so the album was called "Bee Gees 1st". It was their first album to be released internationally.

The album is considered psychedelic rock. If you check out the cover, you'll see the band standing behind what looks like a group of flowers each of which spell out the name of the album and other designs. It was perfect for the late Sixties. Two new musicians were brought in to make the Bee Gees a complete band. Colin Peterson on drums and Vince Melouney on lead guitar. Both were from Australia.

All of the recordings that the Bee Gees did over the next five years or so were done at the International Broadcasting Company (IBC) Studios on Portland Place in London. The finest of British rock recorded at IBC, including Cream, Deep Purple, the Kinks, Rod

Stewart and the Rolling Stones. Even the Beatles recorded a live performance at IBC in 1964.

"Bee Gees 1st" contains their first three hits plus eleven other songs all of which were written by Barry and Robin together or singly. The album reached number seven in the United States and number eight in England, but did even better in France where it was number two.

"Holiday", the third single from the album was not released in England. Instead the single "World" which was from their next album "Horizontal" was released in England, but not in the United States. I don't pretend to understand why the recording labels choose one song for this country and another for another country. I'm sure there are reasons behind it. I just listened to "World" and it is a wonderful ballad. I don't remember ever hearing this song before. I bet it would have been a hit in the U.S. if they had given it a chance.

"World" reached number nine in the United Kingdom.

"Holiday" was a strong hit in the U.S., getting about the same audience as the first two songs. It peaked at number 16 in the U.S., did not chart in England (naturally), but did well in other countries, like the Netherlands where it peaked at number 3.

"(THE LIGHTS WENT OUT IN) MASSACHUSETTS"

Work on "Horizontal" was started in late 1967. They quickly released their first (and only) single from the album in the United States, "(The Lights Went Out in) Massachusetts". Robin sang lead on this song. "Massachusetts" became their first number one record in England. It did well in the United States, too, becoming their highest ranking song to date and peaking at number 11. It was number one in four other countries as well, Germany, New Zealand, Netherlands and Canada.

"Massachusetts" ultimately became one of the best-selling songs of all time, selling over five million copies. It was certainly the biggest selling song of the Bee Gees career. Oddly enough, none of the Bee Gees had actually been to Massachusetts when they recorded the song. Maurice said they just liked the sound of the word. Also, even though Massachusetts is in the United States, the song only reached number 11 here and easily hit number one in several other countries.

"Horizontal" has been called their "heaviest" album. The tone of the music is less frivolous and more somber. Some say, this was in part due to the influence of the two new members of the Bee Gees, Colin Peterson and Vince Melouney. The album reached number 16 in England and number 12 in the United States.

Their popularity was finally catching up to them and in late 1967; the group appeared on the Ed Sullivan Show and Rowan & Martin's Laugh-In. These were their first appearances in America.

They next released a couple singles which were not tied to any album. "Words" was released as a single in early 1968 and did fairly well. It reached number 15 in the United States and number eight in the U.K. The other single "Jumbo" failed to make the Top 40 in the United

States, but got to 25 in England. Both songs can be found on later compilations of their hits, but did not appear on an album in 1968.

Their next album was "Idea", released in September, 1968. This is an interesting album. The version that was released in the U.K. had a song on it called "Such a Shame". This song was the only song on any Bee Gees album that was not written by a Gibb brother. It was written by their lead guitarist, Vince Melouney. Through the magic of YouTube or if you have a later CD version of the album "Idea" which includes the song, you can listen to it.

Vince is doing the guitar and the lead vocals on this song. Barry and Robin do not appear on the song at all.

In the version of the album that was released in the United States, "Such a Shame" was replaced by "I've Gotta Get a Message to You" which became a big hit over here. It reached number eight in the U.S. and even though it wasn't on the U.K. album, it was released as a single there and they got their second number one hit in the U.K.

All three of the brothers are credited for writing "I've Gotta Get a Message to You", but Robin takes the lead vocals on it. The song was written about a man on death row who is about to go to the electric chair and he is pleading with the prison chaplain to get a message to his wife. It's not mentioned in the song, but Robin claims that the prisoner had killed his wife's lover. This all came after Robin had had a argument with his wife and was feeling bad about it.

"I Started a Joke"

Another song on the "Idea" album is a particular favorite of mine. "I Started a Joke" was only released in the United States even though it appears on both versions of the album. It reached number six here in the States. The song was mainly written by Robin, but credit is given to all three. The song would be the highest ranking song of their career up to this point in the United States, peaking at number six. I have to admit, this is one of my favorite Bee Gees songs. If you have ever felt like an outsider, you can relate to this song.

"I started a joke which started the whole world crying". But, it turns out, the joke was on me. Barry said that the song can mean anything you want it to mean. Some say it is about the devil. Years later when Robin passed away, his son, Robin-John, after all the mourners had left, found "I Started a Joke" on YouTube on his cell phone and played it for his father, pressing the phone to his chest in the casket. "I finally died, which started the whole world living". It chokes me up to write this. A great, great Bee Gees song.

In 1969, cracks started to appear in the Bee Gees. Robin felt that their producer, Robert Stigwood was favoring Barry as the lead singer. I find that hard to understand since almost all of the hits that people were hearing on the radio were fronted by Robin.

The next album was to be a concept album called "Masterpiece", but after some discussion, they decided to release a double album, the first one they had done, called "Odessa". "Odessa" would be the last album with the players that had been with them for several years. After recording several songs, Vince Melouney left the band. It was an amicable departure. Vince wanted to play more blues music and joined the band Fanny Adams.

Then there was some argument about which song would be released as the first single from the album. Robin wanted the single "Lamplight", which he sang lead on, to be the first single. Instead, it was decided that "First of May" would be the single, which featured Barry as the lead with "Lamplight" as the B-side of the record. Robin was very upset and left the group.

No one knows if "Lamplight" would have done better than "First of May" as a single, but "First of May" was a very weak hit, only peaking at number 37 on the Billboard Top 40 charts. It did do better in England, peaking at number six.

I am a follower of the single hits more so than the albums. I grew up listening to the radio and following the Top 40 and that is where my love of music originates. However, I realize that most people look upon the work of an artist to include everything they recorded, even if it was never heard on the radio. "Odessa" is rated, by the critics as one of the best albums that the Bee Gees recorded during their career. And yet, it only produced one weak single.

SPLIT UP FOR A WHILE

Robin went off on his own for a while, recording an album, "Robin's Reign" that included a single "Saved by the Bell" which did pretty well in Europe. It was a number two song in England and number one in several other countries, but failed to make much of a mark in the United States, only getting to 87.

Barry and Maurice kept going as the Bee Gees. What were once five was now three and they started work on their next album, "Cucumber Castle". The music from this album was taken from a television special the Bee Gees put together for British television. You can't find much good to say about this film except that it is funny in parts and an all-around family film. It stars Barry and Maurice and the British singer Lulu. It is set in medieval times and the review I read of the film reminded me of some of the stuff Monty Python did.

It was during this period that Colin Petersen, their drummer, was fired. There is some controversy as to why, exactly, he was fired. One story I read was that he had just lost interest in the band. He started missing recording sessions and one source says that he refused to act in the movie "Cucumber Castle". However, I have read that Colin did appear in some scenes in the movie which were later edited out when he was fired.

Colin says the main reason was that Robert Stigwood just didn't like him. Since Colin was an original partner in the corporation known as the Bee Gees, he sued for his share of the company. It was in litigation for years and at one point, Colin told the court that the group did not have the right to the name, Bee Gees. The suit was finally settled, but Colin didn't win. He says that he and the Gibb brothers remained friends and that his beef was mainly with Robert Stigwood.

When Colin left the group, there were just two, Barry and Maurice. They finished "Cucumber Castle" with a new drummer and then parted ways. They released several singles from "Cucumber Castle". One song, "Don't Forget to Remember" did very well in the United Kingdom, peaking at number two, but barely cracked the Top 100 in the United States. Two other songs, "I.O.I.O" and "If I Only Had My Mind on Something Else" did not make any chart.

It seemed the Bee Gees were done. Their popularity was waning, Robin and Colin and Vince had left. In December, 1969, Barry and Maurice decided to call it quits and for a time, the Bee Gees did not exist.

On September 1, 1970, (which was his 24th birthday), Barry married Linda Gray who was a model and the former Miss Edinburgh. They have had five children, Stephen (born 1973), Ashley (born 1977), Travis (born 1981), Michael (born 1984) and Alexandra (born 1991). They are still married.

SOLO PERIOD

Robin, of course, had already left the group and recorded his own solo project "Robin Reigns". In July, 1970, he got together with Maurice and they worked together for a while, but soon realized that they missed Barry. So, they contacted him and decided to work out their differences.

Working solo, Robin had recorded enough to fill a second album. It was called "Sing Slowly Sisters", but was never released.

Maurice also worked on a solo album during this time period. He called it "The Loner", but, again, it was never released. He played most of the instruments and sang all of the parts on the album. While the album was never released, he did release a single from it called "Railroad", but the single didn't really make an impression.

Remember the British singer Lulu? She did very well in England in the Sixties. She had a number one song, "To Sir with Love" which is the theme song of the movie with the same name starring Sidney Poitier. In 1969, she and Maurice Gibb were married. She had acted in the television film "Cucumber Castle". This was a tough time for Maurice and he was drinking heavily. The marriage did not go well and they were divorced in 1973. They did not have any children.

Barry disapproved of the marriage from the beginning, saying that Maurice was too young. This is strange because Robin was the exact same age as Maurice and he had been married at this point for a year or so.

Maurice married again on October 17, 1975 to Yvonne Spenceley. She was working at a club where the group was performing and Maurice was smitten right away. They would have two children,

Adam (born 1976) and Samantha (born 1980) and stay married until his death in 2003. They renewed their wedding vows in 1992.

Maurice might have gotten the acting bug when doing "Cucumber Castle" because he decided to try stage acting in the spring of 1970. He took part in "Sing a Rude Song", a musical that played for 71 shows in London in 1970. It's quite a bit different than what you would expect from a Bee Gees.

Like the others, Barry also started on a solo album. He wrote and recorded many songs during this period and, like Maurice, he released a single. It was called "I'll Kiss Your Memory" and would have been included in the album, "The Kid's No Good". But, unfortunately, the single did nothing and the album was never released.

REUNITED

Robin and Maurice got back together first and recorded "Sincere Relations" and "Lay It On Me". These two songs would later appear on the album "2 Years On" which was their first album after the reunion.

Realizing that they really needed to work together, that going solo just didn't work, the three brothers got back together in late 1970. An Australian drummer, Geoff Bridgford joined the group and now they were four again.

The break must have been good for them, their first single release after the reunion was "Lonely Days" which would peak at number 3 on the U.S. charts, the best showing they had had up to this point. In England, they were a little slower to welcome them back and the song only reached number 33.

Next the group released their first number one song in the United States, "How Do You Mend a Broken Heart" in mid-1971. It was included on the album "Trafalgar". The Bee Gees were doing great in the United States, but not so much in England, where the song did not chart at all.

In 1971, a movie was released called "Melody" which featured several of the Bee Gees songs. The movie, also known as "S.W.A.L.K." (Sealed with a Loving Kiss) in the United Kingdom, did not do well in England or in the United States, but for some reason, they loved it in Japan.

After having a number one in the U.S., they seemed to run out of steam again. In 1972, they recorded three singles, two of which were from the "To Whom It May Concern" album and the third was a single without an album. "My World" which was not on any album at the time (it was included on later greatest hits albums) peaked at number 16 in the United States and England, both. It is a really nice ballad which spotlights the harmonies of the brothers. This was the last hit that included drummer Geoff Bridgford. He did some work on the album and then departed the group. He was replaced on tour by Chris Karan and by other drummers during recording.

"Run To Me" was released next in August, 1972. It was from the album "To Whom It May Concern". The single also reached number 16 in the United States, but did much better in England, peaking at number nine.

The last hit the Bee Gees had in the United States for 2 and a half years was "Alive" also from the "To Whom It May Concern" album. It only reached number 34 in the U.S. and did not chart in England.

To the listener, it seemed as if the Bee Gees disappeared. They were recording and releasing music, but nothing was working. In 1975, Eric Clapton encouraged them to move to Miami, Florida and record there. They put together a new band with Alan Kendall on lead guitar, Dennis Byron on drums and Blue Weaver on keyboards. They were attempting to create a live band that would sound like their studio work. They were also working with record producer Arif Mardin, who worked with hundreds of different acts during the Seventies and Eighties and beyond. They also switched to RSO Records

"JIVE TALKIN'"

Disco was just getting started in the U.S. Some say that "The Hustle" by Van McCoy was the first Disco song, but that's probably up for debate. At any rate, Mardin and Stigwood, their producers convinced the brothers that they should try Disco. The result was "Jive Talkin'" which is considered by many to be their comeback song. They hadn't hit the Top 10 in the United States since 1971 and that was their first number one "How Do You Mend a Broken Heart".

After a four year break from the Top 10, they went right back to number one with "Jive Talkin'" The song was originally called "Drive Talkin" and is modeled after the noise their car made as it crossed the Julia Tuttle Causeway in Miami. When Barry changed the name, producer Mardin asked him if he knew what the term meant. Barry said that, yea, it had to do with dancing. Mardin told him, no, it was black slang term for "bullshitting". Barry was surprised, but said, it is music. You can do anything you want with music.

The song reached number one in the U.S. and Canada and number five in England. It was the first time Barry Gibb would use falsetto in a song.

At any rate, just like they did back in 1967 with "New York Mining Disaster", the record was delivered to radio stations with a blank white cover. The D.J. didn't know what he was playing until he took it out of the sleeve. To my knowledge, there was no backlash from the title of the song. The song was included on their album "Main Course" which also included two other hits (at least in the United States). "Nights on Broadway" was the second single from "Main Course" and the falsetto was very apparent in this song. Mardin asked Barry "Can you scream?" Barry said sure. He then asked; can you scream in tune with the music? Well, of course he could and you hear the results in "Nights on Broadway". The song reached number seven in the United States which made two top 10 songs back to back. That hadn't happened since 1968.

The third single from "Main Course" didn't do as well as the first two, but is one of my favorite Bee Gees songs. "Fanny (Be Tender with My Love)" was released in January, 1976 and peaked at number 12 in the U.S., but did not chart in the U.K.

"CHILDREN OF THE WORLD"

Once Barry found out that the world liked the falsetto singing, he used it in everything. That really became the "sound" of the Bee Gees in the late Seventies. Their next album was "Children of the World", which also produced three hit singles and the album itself reached number eight in the U.S., but, again, did not chart in England.

The first single from "Children" was "You Should Be Dancing" which perpetuated the Disco theme and emphasized Barry's falsetto again. This was another number one song for the guys in the United States. In England, it hit number five which is amazing considering the last two singles did not chart there at all.

The Bee Gees really had a new sound. This was much different than the music from the Sixties. Some fans didn't like it and deserted them, but they picked up so many new fans that it made up for it. In fact, it was "Children of the World" that really pushed them into super-stardom. I remember the Seventies and hearing the new sound for the first time. I loved it and still do. I have always been a big Disco fan. Later, in the Eighties, when it was said that "Disco was dead", it wasn't for me. I continued to like Disco and still do.

Two more hits came from the "Children" album. "Love So Right" featured more of Barry's falsetto and peaked at number three in the United States. It didn't do quite as well in England, reaching number 41. By now, the black listening community had noticed the Bee Gees and they were starting to appear on the R&B charts (at this time it was called the Billboard Black Singles Charts). "Love So Right" reached number 27 on the Black charts.

This song was really in the same style as their Sixties material, but the falsetto brought it up to date and gave it a whole new sound.

The third hit was "Boogie Child". This song reached number 12 on the Billboard Top 40 charts. Once again, however, the song did not chart in England.

"SATURDAY NIGHT FEVER"

It was time for a live album. "Here at Last…Bee Gees" was their sixteenth album and the first live album of their career. It was released in May, 1977. It contains most of their early hits, and a couple new songs. "Edge of the Universe" was released from the album and did pretty well in Canada and the United States, peaking at number 26, here. As far as I can tell, this is their only live song to reach the singles charts.

Later in November, 1977, the album for the movie "Saturday Night Fever" was released. The movie starred John Travolta. This wasn't Travolta's first movie, but it was his breakthrough film. The film was made using other music that Travolta could dance to. The film was in post-production when they decided they needed new music for the movie. Their producer, Robert Stigwood asked the Bee Gees to write the music. They hid out in France at the Château d'Hérouville studio and literally wrote all of the songs in a weekend.

The "Saturday Night Fever" album stayed at the top on the album charts for 24 consecutive weeks, from January until June of 1978. It then fell out of number one, but stayed on the album charts for a total of 120 weeks, finally falling out in 1980. It also spent 18 weeks at number one on the album charts in England.

While "Saturday Night Fever" did not define Disco, it certainly helped keep it alive for several more years than it might have without the film. Everyone was in love with the film. I know I, at one point, had two or three different versions of the soundtrack. I know I had the vinyl, and later bought the cassette and then finally the CD when it became available.

In 2010, it was announced that, with over 40 million copies sold, the album was the fourth bestselling album of all time. Rolling Stone magazine has rated it number 131 of the 500 Greatest Albums of All Time. It won a Grammy in 1979 for Album of the Year.

The Bee Gees wrote most of the music for "Saturday Night Fever", but gave away some of the songs to other people. The songs that the guys held for themselves were "Stayin' Alive", "How Deep Is Your Love" and "Night Fever". They also wrote "If I Can't Have You" which is sung by Yvonne Elliman" in the movie and was a number one song for Elliman. Also "More Than a Woman" can be heard in the movie in two different versions, one by the Bee Gees and one by Tavares. The Tavares version reached number 32 on the Billboard singles charts.

It is weird that "Jive Talkin'" and "You Should Be Dancing" were also included on the soundtrack, but never appeared in the movie itself.

"How Deep Is Your Love"

"How Deep Is Your Love" was the first of six number one hits the Bee Gees would have, consecutively in 1978 and 1979. It was originally written for Yvonne Elliman for the movie, but the guys decided to record it themselves. It hit number one in the U.S. and Canada and number three in England. The song is ranked number 20 on Billboard magazine's All Time Top 100. Rolling Stone placed it at number 366 on its list of the 500 Greatest Songs of All Time. In 1983, the boys were sued by a Chicago song writer named Ronald Selle who claimed they had stolen the melody for "How Deep is Your Love" from his song "Let It End". At first the jury decided in favor of Mr. Selle, but it was later overturned.

"Stayin' Alive" was the second of three songs from the movie that hit number one. It was number four in England. Unfortunately, during the recording of this song, the mother of Dennis Byron, their drummer passed away. This meant Dennis was unavailable for a time. Now, they were in France at the time and drummers were hard to come by. So, rather than hire a new drummer, they selected two bars from the song "Night Fever" which had already been recorded and put those two bars on an infinite loop and the two bars play over and over and over throughout the song. The rhythm is unchanging through the entire song.

They then listed the drummer on the single as "Bernard Lupe" which is a parody of a real drummer named Bernard Purdie. The services of Mr. Lupe were sought after for quite a while until it was revealed that he did not exist. An interesting piece of trivia is that "Stayin' Alive" has close to 104 beats per minute, which makes it an ideal song to use to practice CPR. The compression rate of the chest during CPR should be between 100-120 beats per minute. So, if you are doing CPR, think of "Stayin' Alive" in your mind and you'll have the correct number of compressions.

"Night Fever", was actually recorded first for the album, but released third. It also hit number one (the third in a row) and stayed there for eight weeks. "Night Fever" was also number one in England. This was third of four number one songs written by the Gibbs that consecutively held the number one spot for 15 weeks from February, 1978 until late May, 1979. The first was "Stayin' Alive"; it was followed by "(Love is) Thicker than Water" by the younger Gibb brother, Andy Gibb. Even though the Bee Gees didn't sing on the record, Barry wrote it for Andy. "Thicker than Water" was replaced by "Night Fever" which was replaced by "If I Can't Have You" by Yvonne Elliman which, of course, Barry also wrote.

Actually, if you consider the entire period from just before Christmas, 1977 until summer of 1978, a 32 week period, 25 of those weeks was held by a song that was written by the Gibb brothers. And, as a bonus, Barry and Robin also wrote a song for an old friend of theirs from Australia, Samantha Sang. The song "Emotion", while not a number one, did peak at number three in the United States in early 1978. The Bee Gees were on fire.

If you count "Emotion" (and I'm counting it), the Bee Gees were responsible for five of the Top 10 songs during March, 1978. That hadn't been done since the Beatles did it in 1964. Also, Barry had written or co-wrote four consecutive number ones which broke the record of Paul McCartney and John Lennon. Barry remains to this day the only person to have written four consecutive number ones.

John Travolta went from one huge movie with great music to another one. "Grease" came out in June of 1978 and starred Travolta and Olivia Newton-John. Now as much as I like "Saturday Night Fever", "Grease" became my new favorite movie of all time and has pretty much remained at that spot throughout my life. The title song for

"Grease", recorded by Frankie Valli of the Four Seasons was written by Barry Gibb. This gave him yet another number one in the United States.

In mid-1978, the guys got involved with a movie that was being made to honor the Beatles. "Sgt. Pepper's Lonely Hearts Club Band" starred Peter Frampton and the Bee Gees and contained music that had previously been done by the Beatles. The film has been called "disjointed" and was panned by the critics. The public just sort of ignored it. So, after being on the top of the world for a few months, they were brought back to earth by this film. The only song to make a dent in the charts was the cover of "Oh, Darling" which was recorded by Robin alone without his brothers. It peaked at number 15 in the U.S.

"SPIRITS HAVING FLOWN"

Upon completion of the "Saturday Night Fever" album, they got right to work on a new album. This one would be called "Spirits Having Flown". It would result in three more number one songs, which would mean six number ones in a row by the group. This had never been done before and would not be done again until the mid-Eighties when Whitney Houston would have seven number ones consecutively.

The three songs, "Too Much Heaven", "Tragedy" and "Love You Inside Out" would almost mark the end of the Bee Gees, at least on the charts.

"Too Much Heaven" was written as a contribution to the "Music for UNICEF Concert" that was held at the United Nations in January, 1979. The Bee Gees donated the entire royalties from the song to UNICEF which eventually amounted to about $11 million. I mentioned it was number one in the U.S. It was also number three in the United Kingdom. Because of this generous donation to UNICEF, President Jimmy Carter invited the guys to the White House where he thanked them in person.

"Tragedy" was next at the top of the charts. This song actually reached number one in England before it did in the United States. It also was number one in Canada, Spain, France, Ireland, Italy, New Zealand and Brazil. If you listen to this song, you'll hear several "explosions" near the end. To me, it sounds like thunder or a gun being fired. But, this sound-effect was created by Barry, just using his voice and mouth. He made the sound into a microphone and then the sound was layered upon itself and mixed until they got the sound they wanted.

In 1998, a five-person British group called Steps recorded their version of "Tragedy" and it also went to number one in England.

Check it out on YouTube. It's a pretty good version of the song (no explosions, though).

Barry, Maurice and Robin wrote "Tragedy" and "Too Much Heaven" on an afternoon break from working on the "Sgt. Peppers" album. Then, the same day they wrote "Shadow Dancing" for their brother Andy Gibb. To those of us without that kind of talent, it's hard to fathom just how someone can sit down and write three songs in an afternoon and they are all great.

Released in mid-1979, "Love You Inside Out" was the last hit by the Bee Gees to hit the top of the charts, but it did set several records. It was the sixth consecutive number one by a group. No one had done that. There is some claim that the Beatles did it, but that was in England, not in America, so the Bee Gees held the record for the United States until Whitney Houston came along. At the time, this placed them fourth among all artists with number ones and in total weeks at number one (27).

Bee Gees fever was hot in the world in 1979. So, obviously, a tour was in order. The tour started in Fort Worth, Texas and then covered 41 dates, ending in Miami, Florida where they all lived. Their younger brother, Andy, would join them on stage during the number "You Should Be Dancing" which is as close as Andy came to being a Bee Gee himself. Also, during the Houston, Texas concert, they had a surprise visit from John Travolta who came on stage and performed some of his dance moves from "Saturday Night Fever".

The guys even hit the country charts in the U.S. The B-side of "Too Much Heaven", called "Rest Your Love on Me" just broke into the Top 40, peaking at number 39. But that's enough for an entry in the Country Top 40 book. Conway Twitty, one of the biggest country artists of all time, covered the song in 1981 and reached number one.

DISCO IS DEAD

Unfortunately, the Bee Gees were totally connected to the Disco dance craze, which was extremely popular in the late Seventies. But people, being fickle, can change on a dime and in mid-1979, Disco suddenly fell out of favor with the record buying public. "Disco sucks" and "death to Disco" where heard everywhere. I have never understood how sentiment can change so fast. Styles of music or particular performers have lost favor several times over the history of rock and roll and I am perplexed each time it happens. If music was good yesterday, why isn't it good today?

The day Disco died is pretty much recognized as July 12, 1979 when a "Disco Demolition Night" was held between two Chicago White Sox games at Comiskey Park in Chicago. The event, which included destroying records, caused a riot among the fans that were there for the game and the second game had to be forfeited. The next Billboard chart came out on July 21, nine days later, and it showed that Disco songs held the top six spots on the charts. Two months later, by mid-September, there were no Disco songs on the charts. It had disappeared that fast.

Now, Disco didn't die immediately, there were some songs into the Eighties and Nineties that could be called Disco, and eventually, a "Dance" category was created for Billboard and what used to be called Disco, could now be called dance and everyone was happy.

The death of Disco pretty much signaled the death of the Bee Gees. But they would not leave. They kept at it, writing and recording for themselves and others. In 1980, Barry teamed up with Barbra Streisand and wrote or co-wrote (with his brothers) all nine of the songs on her new album, "Guilty". It turned out to be Streisand's best-selling album to date, selling over 12 million copies and peaking at number one on the album charts in the U.S., England and several other countries. I particularly like the cover which shows Barry and Barbra all in white, Barry embracing Barbra.

The first song released from the album, written by Barry and Robin, but performed by just Barbra Streisand was "Woman in Love" which spent three weeks at number one in the U.S. The title song "Guilty" a duet between Barry and Barbra reached number three on the U.S. charts and number 34 in the U.K. "Guilty" also won a Grammy for Best Pop Vocal Performance, Duo or Group.

In February, 1981, they released a second duet, "What Kind of Fool" which peaked at number ten on the U.S. charts.

In 1981, the Bee Gees recorded another album, "Living Eyes", but it was not a success, only selling 750,000 copies as opposed to "Spirits Having Flown" which sold over 30 million copies. An interesting piece of trivia about this album is it is the very first album to be played on the air in CD form. We think of CD's as common place today, but in 1981, they hadn't yet begun. A BBC show called "Tomorrow's World" played the CD of "Living Eyes" over the air, making it the first.

THE BEE GEES START TO FADE AWAY

This would be their last album on the RSO label. They released a couple singles from the album, but only "He's a Liar" hit the charts, coming in at a weak number 30. The radio stations were still reacting to the death of Disco and pretty much had stopped playing anything by the Bee Gees.

Barry kept writing for others. In 1982, Dionne Warwick had a hit, "Heartbreaker", which was mostly written by the Bee Gees. A year later, in 1983, Kenny Rogers and Dolly Parton had a huge hit, "Islands in the Stream", which went to number one. It was written by Barry. In fact, the entire album that contains that song was written by the brothers and produced by Barry Gibb.

Considering the way the public felt about Disco, it's strange to me that in 1983, they filmed a sequel to "Saturday Night Fever" starring John Travolta, again. This new one was "Staying Alive" and featured the Bee Gees song as the title song. The brothers also contributed a lot of music to the film, but it was nothing like "Saturday Night Fever". They got one hit out of it, "The Woman in You" which peaked at number 24 in May, 1983.

Continuing to work for others, they wrote an album for Diana Ross, "Eaten Alive", in which Michael Jackson is listed as a co-writer on the title track. The song from the album, "Chain Reaction", went to number one in England and in Australia, but did not chart in the United States.

So, the Bee Gees were still charting, but no one knew about it unless you read the liner notes. The Gibbs released another album, "E.S.P." in 1987. It did very well for them, although not on the same scale as previous albums. It was their first album on the Warner Bros. Label and was also the first album they recorded digitally. The album sold well in Europe and the United Kingdom, but did very little in the U.S., barely cracking the Top 100. One single from the album "You Win Again" reached number one in England, but only got to number 75 in the U.S.

Robin Gibb had divorced his first wife, Molly, in 1980. He then married author and artist Dwina Murphy and he would stay married to her for the rest of his life. They had one son together, Robin-John Gibb, born on January 23, 1983. Robin had one additional child, a daughter named Snow Evelyn Robin Juliet Gibb who was born in 2008 through a relationship he had with a housekeeper, Clair Yang.

THE LOSS OF ANDY GIBB

On March 10, 1988, their youngest brother, Andy, died of myocarditis which is an inflammation of the heart muscle usually caused by a virus in the body. It was commonly felt among the Gibb family that Andy's use of drugs and alcohol was a major contributor to his early death. He was 30 years old.

The brothers had talked about bringing Andy into the group and making him an official Bee Gees member. Andy would have brought a new element to the group and maybe a little different sound and maybe kick-start their career again. But, alas, it was not to be.

Maurice was a recovering alcoholic at this time. The death of his brother hit him hard and he found himself relapsing. It took him a long time to become completely sober. At one point, it became so bad that he actually threatened his wife and children with a gun. This incident acted like a wakeup call to Maurice and he re-committed himself to quitting.

Their next album, "One", released in 1989 was dedicated to Andy. It's a shame he couldn't have sung on it. The album is very low-key and you can hear the influence of Andy's death in their music. The title song, "One" was the only single from the album to chart, but it put the Bee Gees back in the Top 10, peaking at number seven. This was the first time they were in the Top 10 since the good old days of 1979, ten years before.

The Nineties were not that good to the Bee Gees. They kept recording albums. "High Civilization" came out in 1991 and reached 24 in the U.K., but did not chart in the United States. Next was "Size Isn't Everything", in 1993, which repeated the previous album, peaking at number 23 in England, but stalling at number 153 in the United States.

They did a little better in 1997 with "Still Waters" which peaked at number two in the United Kingdom and reached number 11 in the U.S. The one single from "Still Waters" was "Alone" which did well, considering. It reached number five in England and number 28 in the United States. Unfortunately, this would be the last single the Bee Gees would chart in the United States. Their career seemed to be over.

Well, not quite. On February 24, 1997, they were awarded the Outstanding Contribution to Music Award at the Brit Awards. In November, they played Las Vegas with a show called "One Night Only" and that was all it was supposed to be, one night. Barry had been having some problems with arthritis, which made it difficult to perform sometimes. It was announced that because of Barry's health problems, this would be the last live performance for the Bee Gees. The response from the audience was so positive and so many copies of the CD of the concert were sold (5 million) that they decided to take the concert on tour despite the problems Barry was having.

In 1998, they recorded a song with Celine Dion called "Immortality" which is on her album, "Let's Talk about Love". The song did not chart, however.

The tour went on, however. The "One Night Only" tour started in Las Vegas, then played Wembley Stadium in London in September 1998 and concluded at the Olympic Stadium in Sydney, Australia in March 1999.

On December 31, 1999, the last day of the century, the guys played what would be their last full concert. Called BG2K, they performed, back home, at Sunrise, Florida to a sold-out crowd. When the clock struck 12 and a new century started, the people were dancing to the sounds of the Bee Gees.

In 2001, they recorded what would be their last album together. "This is Where I Came In" was released in April and marked the fifth decade that the Bee Gees had recorded together. The album did well, peaking at number six in England and number 16 in the United States. The one single from the album, the title song, did well in England, reaching number 18, but did not chart in the U.S. This would be the last Bee Gees single to chart anywhere.

In 2005, Barry and Linda Gibb bought the former home of Johnny Cash in Hendersonville, Tennessee. Barry had the idea that he would restore the home and turn it into a songwriting retreat. Unfortunately, the home caught fire in 2007 and was completely destroyed.

MAURICE

In early January of 2003, Maurice started feeling intense stomach pains. He was admitted to the Mount Sinai Medical Center in Miami, Florida and prepared for surgery. He was diagnosed with a twisted intestine. But before the surgery could be started, he had a heart attack. The first attack did not kill him, however, so the surgeons decided to go ahead with the operation.

On January 12, 2003, he suddenly had a second heart attack and died. He was 53 years old. Barry and Robin were devastated over the loss. At first, they resolved to carry on with the name, the Bee Gees, but it soon became apparent that their heart just wasn't in it. So, they officially retired the name, the Bee Gees.

There was some talk of a malpractice suit against the doctors because the family didn't believe they had acted appropriately. But nothing ever came of it.

Nearly 200 people attended the funeral of Maurice Gibb, including Michael Jackson. Some sources say that, Maurice was cremated and others say he is interred in a cemetery in Miami, Florida..

A month or so later, the brothers received the Grammy Legend Award. This is an award to individuals or bands who have contributed significantly to the field of recording. The first award was given in 1994 and, as far as I can determine, the last one that has been given was to the Bee Gees in 2003. It has not been awarded since then.

Barry and Robin appeared along with Maurice's son Adam, to tearfully accept the award. The guys had already started on solo projects again. Robin's solo "Magnet" was released the same week Maurice died. In 2004, he embarked on a tour of Europe and Asia, doing his solo work.

In 2005, Barry got together again with Barbra Streisand to do "Guilty Pleasures", a follow-up to "Guilty". It was actually called "Guilty II" in Europe. The album did fairly well for Barbra, but nothing like the first album, peaking at number five on the album charts.

Barry and Robin reunited for a Charity concert in February, 2006. There was talk of them getting together again and reforming the Bee Gees, but nothing ever came of it. In 2009, in a radio interview, Barry made the statement that "they will be back"

In 2010, it was announced that a biopic was being planned by director Steven Spielberg to do the life story of the Bee Gees. Barry and Robin would work as technical advisors and actors would play the brothers. The problem was duplicating the music. Would the actors try to emulate the sound or would they do voice-overs. No decision was made and, to my knowledge, no movie was ever made.

ROBIN

In August, 2010, Robin began to have stomach pains. He was immediately taken to a hospital where he was diagnosed with a twisted intestine, the same thing that killed his brother, Maurice. Robin, however, was operated on and soon recovered.

In November of 2011, it was announced that Robin had been diagnosed with liver cancer. He was 61 years old at the time. He had grown visibly thinner over the previous months and rumors had started. Several concerts had to be cancelled due to his health. On February 13, 2012, he joined with a trio of British military officers who called themselves The Soldiers for a charity concert at London Palladium. This would be his last public appearance.

On April 14, 2012, Robin came down with pneumonia and was admitted into a hospital in Chelsea. He quickly lapsed into a coma. Then, a week or so later, he came out of the coma, but his physical health had deteriorated a great deal. He never recovered from the ordeal and on May 20, 2012, Robin Gibb passed away.

Robin's son Robin-John felt it important to note that Robin did not die of cancer, which is what started his downhill slide. He, in fact, died of kidney and liver failure. His passing was "dignified and peaceful".

Robin was buried in Thame, Oxfordshire, England. His mother, Barbara, was still alive at 92 and was wheelchair bound at the services. Also attending were his wife, Dwina and his sons Spencer and RJ (Robin-John). Robin's coffin was brought into the cemetery accompanied by the sounds of "How Deep Is Your Love". Dwina read a short poem which she had written herself called "My Songbird Has Flown".

After the service, Robin was laid to rest in the St. Mary's Church graveyard, just a few yards from a memorial to his younger brother, Andy.

A formal memorial was held later in September, 2012 in London to honor Robin.

The Bee Gees were officially over. Barry Gibb is now the last surviving member.

LEGACY OF THE BEE GEES

The Bee Gees have sold over 200 Million records worldwide. At one point in time, they were responsible in some way for nine of the songs in the Billboard Top 100. They are also the most successful trio in pop history.

They are the only artists of the past 50 years to score a number one hit in each of four decades, Sixties, Seventies, Eighties and Nineties.

The Guinness Book of World Records lists Barry Gibb as the second most successful songwriter in history, right after Paul McCartney.

More than 2500 artists have recorded Bee Gees songs. These include Michael Bolton, Eric Clapton, Elton John and many, many more.

In 1979, the trio got their official star on the Hollywood Walk of Fame. It's located at 6845 Hollywood Blvd.

In 1994, they were inducted into the Songwriter's Hall of Fame.

Three years later, in 1997, they were inducted into the Rock & Roll Hall of Fame. Brian Wilson of the Beach Boys presented them their award. That same year they were inducted into ARIA (Australian Recording Industry Association). They have also joined the Vocal Group Hall of Fame, the Dance Music Hall of Fame and London's Walk of Fame.

1997 was a big year for the Bee Gees. That was the year they received the Legend Award from the World Music Awards, which is usually held in Monte Carlo, Monaco to honor world-wide performers who experience unusual world-wide sales.

In 1997, they also won the Brit Award for Outstanding Contribution to Music.

The American Music Awards were started in 1974 by Dick Clark and go on to this day. The Bee Gees won an award on this show in 1979, 1980 and 1997.

I thought this was cool: After the huge success of "Saturday Night Fever", the governor of Florida named the three honorary citizens of Florida.

Like the Beatles and others before them, the Bee Gees were appointed Commanders in the Order of the British Empire (CBE) by Queen Elizabeth on May 27, 2004. Maurice was awarded posthumously.

Only five other performers have outsold the Bee Gees. They are Elvis Presley, The Beatles, Michael Jackson, Garth Brooks and Paul McCartney.

AFTERWORD

The Bee Gees have been called Britain's first family of harmony. They have been called a chameleon because of the different styles they have sung. No one can deny that they have done it all. Through it all, they have adapted to what the public was listening to at the time and became superstars in the process.

My son told me that the Bee Gees shouldn't be a "Legend of Rock & Roll", instead they should be a "Legend of Disco". I told him I considered Disco, rock and roll and besides the group has been inducted into the Rock & Roll Hall of Fame which makes them eligible for these books.

As I get older and we continue to lose the greats of American and English music, I realize that I am losing my youth and my middle age and my old age and everything in between. Thank goodness the music has been kept and we can go back and listen to it again.

Maurice would be only 64 years old (as of this writing) if he had lived; certainly young enough to give us new music. We lost Robin just last year and he would, of course, also be 64 years old if he were still here. It's ironic that Barry, the oldest, is still with us. But, I'm so glad he is.

You can contact me at www.number1project.com where I occasionally blog about things that interest me in the music world (mostly, the twentieth century). Go find it and read it and leave me a comment. I also have a Facebook fan page called "Legends of Rock & Roll". "Like" me and comment there, too. If you love the music as much as I do, you'll enjoy the trip. Thanks for reading.

I hope you have enjoyed this book as much as I have enjoyed writing it for you.

If you have liked what you read, will you please do me a favor and leave a review of "The Bee Gees". Thank you.

GRAMMY AWARDS

1978 Best Pop Vocal Performance by a Group for "How Deep Is Your Love"

1979 Best Pop Vocal Performance by a Duo or Group and Album of the Year and Producer of the Year for "Saturday Night Fever" and for Best Arrangement of Voices on "Stayin' Alive'

1981 Best Pop Vocal Performance by a Duo or Group with Vocal for "Guilty"

2000 Lifetime Achievement Award

2003 Legend Award

2004 Hall of Fame Award for "Saturday Night Fever"

Selected Discography

Albums

1965 The Bee Gees Sing and Play 14 Barry Gibb Songs

1966 Spicks and Specks

1967 Bee Gees 1st

1968 Horizontal

1968 Idea

1969 Odessa

1970 Cucumber Castle

1970 2 Years On

1971 Trafalgar

1972 To Whom It May Concern

1973 Life in a Tin Can

1974 Mr. Natural

1975 Main Course

1976 Children of the World

1979 Spirits Having Flown

1981 Living Eyes

1987 E.S.P.

1989 One

1991 High Civilization

1993 Size Isn't Everything

1997 Still Waters

2001 This is Where I Came In

Live Albums

1977 Here at Last…Bee Gees…Live

1998 One Night Only

Soundtracks

1971 Melody

1977 Saturday Night Fever

1978 Sgt. Pepper's Lonely Hearts Club Band

1983 Staying Alive

Singles

(Only A-side given in most cases)

1963 "The Battle of the Blue and the Grey" (AUS)

1963 "Timber!" (AUS)

1964 "Peace of Mind" (AUS)

1964 "Claustrophobia" (AUS)

1964 "Turn Around, Look at Me" (AUS)

1965 "Every Day I Have to Cry" (AUS)

1965 "Wine and Women" (AUS)

1965 "I Was A Lover, A Leader Of Men" (AUS)

1966 "I Want Home" (AUS)

1966 "Monday's Rain" (AUS)

Starting here, singles are released to all countries except where noted

1967 "Spicks and Specks"

1967 "New York Mining Disaster 1941"

1967 "To Love Somebody"

1967 "Holiday" (not released in U.K.)

1967 "Massachusetts"

1967 "World" (not released in U.S.)

1968 "Words"

1968 "Jumbo"

1968 "I've Gotta Get a Message to You"

1968 "I Started a Joke" (not released in U.K.)

1969 "First of May"

1969 "Tomorrow Tomorrow"

1969 "Don't Forget to Remember"

1970 "Let There Be Love"

1970 "If Only I Had My Mind on Something Else"

1970 "I.O.I.O."

1970 "Lonely Days"

1971 "Melody Fair

1971 "Han Can You Mend a Broken Heart"

1972 "My World"

1972 "Israel"

1972 "Run to Me"

1972 "Sea of Smiling Faces"

1973 "Saw a New Morning"

1973 "Wouldn't I Be Someone"

1974 "Mr. Natural"

1974 "Throw a Penny"

1974 "Charade"

1975 "Jive Talkin'"

1975 "Nights on Broadway"

1976 "Fanny (Be Tender with My Love)"

1976 "You Should Be Dancing"

1976 "Love So Right"

1977 "Boogie Child"

1977 "Children of the World"

1977 "Edge of the Universe" (Live)

1977 "How Deep is Your Love"

1977 "Stayin' Alive"

1978 "Night Fever"

1978 "More Than a Woman"

1978 "Sgt. Pepper's Lonely Hearts Club Band/With a Little Help from My Friends"

1978 "Too Much Heaven"

1979 "Tragedy"

1979 "Love You Inside Out"

1979 "Spirits (Having Flown)"

1981 "He's a Liar"

1981 "Living Eyes"

1983 "The Woman in You"

1983 "Someone Belonging to Someone"

1987 "You Win Again"

1987 "E.S.P."

1988 "Crazy for Your Love" (released in the U.K.)

1988 "Angela" (not released in the U.K.)

1989 "Ordinary Lives"

1989 "One"

1990 "Bodyguard"

1991 "Secret Love" (not released in the U.S.)

1991 "When He's Gone" (released only in U.S.)

1991 "The Only Love"

1991 "Happy Ever After" (released only in U.S."

1993 "Paying the Price of Love"

1993 "For Whom the Bell Tolls"

1994 "How to Fall in Love, Part 1" (released only in the U.K.)

1994 "Kiss of Life" (not released in the U.K.)

1997 "Alone"

1997 "I Could Not Love You More"

1997 "Still Waters (Run Deep)"

1998 "Immortality"

2001 "This is Where I Came In"

Printed in Great Britain
by Amazon

51392774R10038